## Safety First!

# Safety around Strangers

by Lucia Raatma

## Bridgestone Books

an imprint of Capstone Press
Mankato, Minnesota

Bridgestone Books are published by Capstone Press
818 North Willow Street, Mankato, Minnesota 56001
http://www.capstone-press.com

*Library of Congress Cataloging-in-Publication Data*
Raatma, Lucia.
Safety around strangers/by Lucia Raatma
    p. cm.—(Safety first!)
Includes bibliographical references (p. 24) and index.
Summary: Provides a definition of strangers and ways to be safe around them as well as
suggestions on where to go for help if needed.
ISBN 0-7368-0060-3
1. Safety education—Juvenile literature. 2. Children and strangers—Juvenile literature.
3. Abduction—Prevention—Juvenile literature. [1. Safety. 2. Strangers.
3. Kidnapping—Prevention.] I. Title. II. Series: Raatma, Lucia. Safety first.
HQ770.7.R27 1999
613.6—dc21
                                                                98-22394
                                                                    CIP
                                                                    AC

Capstone Press wishes to thank Judy Kirby at the National Crime Prevention
Council for reviewing this material.

**Editorial Credits**
Rebecca Glaser, editor; Clay Schotzko/Icon Productions, cover designer;
   Sheri Gosewisch, photo researcher

**Photo Credits**
Barbara Stitzer, 4, 6, 8, 10, 12, 14, 16, 18, 20
Leslie O'Shaughnessy, cover

# Table of Contents

## Strangers

A stranger is someone you do not know. You know your family, friends, and teachers. Everyone else is a stranger. Most strangers are good. But some strangers are bad. They might want to hurt you. You must learn to be careful around strangers.

**People You Can Trust**

Many people can help you stay safe from bad strangers. You can trust people such as police officers and fire fighters. Ask your parents which other adults can help you stay safe.

## What Bad Strangers Might Do

Bad strangers might offer you a ride home. They might say your parents asked them to pick you up. They might promise to give you gifts like candy or money. But bad strangers use lies and gifts to trick you. Never take anything from strangers. Say no. Run away and tell an adult you trust.

## What Bad Strangers Might Say

Bad strangers might say things to trick you. They might pretend to be hurt. They might ask you to help find a lost puppy. Say no. Tell an adult you trust if a stranger asks you for help.

## Staying with Groups

Bad strangers usually look for a child who is alone. You can stay safe by going places with other people. Stay with your group at all times. Never go anywhere alone. Ask a good stranger for help if you get lost.

## Safe Routes

A route is the path you follow to go places. Ask your parents to make sure your route is safe. Your parents can show you places along your route to go for help. It is safest to walk where there are many people. Bad strangers could hide near empty lots, parks, or streets.

## Stay Away from Strangers

You may pass by strangers on busy streets or in stores. Try to stay three feet (one meter) away from them. Stay back if a stranger pulls up in a car. A bad stranger could pull you inside the car. Scream for help if someone tries to grab you.

## Never Go with Strangers

You should never go anywhere with strangers. Always say no if strangers ask you to go somewhere. Do not get into strangers' cars. Do not enter strangers' homes. Always check with your parents before you go anywhere.

## Running Away from Strangers

Bad strangers may not leave you alone. Yell for help and make a lot of noise. Tell people the stranger is not your parent. Run into a store or another public place. Ask for help from an adult you trust.

# Hands on: Make a Family Code Word

Strangers might pretend to know your parents. But the strangers may be lying. You can learn to be smarter than strangers. Make a code word with your family.

1. Make up your own family code word. Choose a word that everyone can remember. Choose a word that would be hard to guess.
2. Make sure everyone in your family knows the code word. It must be a secret. Do not tell anyone else your code word.
3. Your parents would use the code word in an emergency. They might have to send another person to pick you up. They will tell that person the code word. That person will tell you the code word.
4. Practice using your code word with your family. Your parents should pretend they are someone else picking you up. They will tell you the code word. Then you know it is safe to go with them.
5. Never go with anyone who does not know your code word. The person should tell you the code word first. Then you will know that your parents sent the person.

# Words to Know

**emergency** (i-MUHR-juhn-see)—a sudden danger

**route** (ROUT)—the path you follow to go somewhere

**stranger** (STRAYN-jur)—anyone you do not know

# Read More

**Boelts, Maribeth.** *A Kid's Guide to Staying Safe on the Streets.* The Kid's Library of Personal Safety. New York: Power Kids Press, 1997.

**Carter, Kyle.** *From Crime.* Safety. Vero Beach, Fla.: Rourke Press, 1994.

**Watson, Carol.** *Run, Yell & Tell!: A Safety Book for Children.* Minneapolis: Missing Children Minnesota, 1993.

# Internet Sites

**Abduction—Protection in Knowledge**
http://kise.simplenet.com/child.html
**Be Street Smart! Be Safe!**
http://www.viasub.net/careful/careful.html

# Index